D1712893

GREAT STORIES OF COURAGE

WORLD ALMANAC® LIBRARY

A note from the editors: These stories reflect many of the values, opinions, and standards of language that existed during the times in which the works were written. Much of the language is also a reflection of the personalities and lifestyles of the stories' narrators and characters. Readers today may strongly disagree, for example, with the ways in which members of various groups, such as women or ethnic minorities, are described or portrayed. In compiling these works, however, we felt that it was important to capture as much of the flavor and character of the original stories as we could and to use art that also captures the spirit of the lives and times of the stories and characters. Rather than delete or alter language that is intrinsically important to literature, we hope that these stories will give parents, educators, and young readers a chance to think and talk about the many ways in which people lead their lives, view the world, and express their feelings about what they have lived through.

Please visit our Web site at: www.garethstevens.com
For a free color catalog describing World Almanac® Library's list of high-quality books and multimedia programs, call 1-800-848-2928 (USA) or 1-800-387-3178 (Canada). World Almanac® Library's fax: (414) 332-3567.

Library of Congress Cataloging-in-Publication Data available upon request from publisher.
Fax (414) 336-0157 for the attention of the Publishing Records Department.

ISBN-13: 978-0-8368-7926-1 (lib. bdg.)
ISBN-13: 978-0-8368-7933-9 (softcover)

This North American edition first published in 2007 by
World Almanac® Library
A Member of the WRC Media Family of Companies
330 West Olive Street, Suite 100
Milwaukee, Wisconsin 53212 USA

World Almanac® Library editorial direction: Mark Sachner
World Almanac® Library editors: Monica Rausch and Tea Benduhn
World Almanac® Library art direction: Tammy West
World Almanac® Library designer: Scott Krall
World Almanac® Library production: Jessica Yanke and Robert Kraus

Printed in Canada

1 2 3 4 5 6 7 8 9 10 10 09 08 07 06

THE RED BADGE OF COURAGE

MY FIRST BATTLE! AM I THE ONLY ONE OUT HERE WHO'S SCARED TO DEATH?
AM I BRAVE ENOUGH TO FIGHT? OR WILL I RUN LIKE A RABBIT?

PAGES 22-38

I'M JIM HAWKINS AND I'LL NEVER FORGET EXACTLY HOW MY WHOLE AMAZING ADVENTURE BEGAN

PAGES 40-56

A BANK STREET CLASSIC TALE
The CALL of the WILD
BY JACK LONDON
ADAPTED BY SEYMOUR REIT
PENCILED BY ERNIE COLÓN
INKED BY BILL WYLIE
COLORED BY JEAN CASEY
LETTERED BY GEORGE ROBERTS
THE MEN OF THE FAR NORTH TELL OF A WILD GHOST DOG WHO RUNS AT THE HEAD OF THE WOLF PACK. THEY SPEAK OF HIM WITH GREAT FEAR, FOR HE IS BRAVE AND CUNNING. HE STEALS THEIR FOOD. HE KILLS THEIR ANIMALS. HE DEFIES THEIR HUNTERS.
WHO IS THIS WILD, MYSTERIOUS GHOST DOG? AND WHY DOES HE RUN WITH THE WOLVES?
OUR STORY BEGINS IN THE YEAR 1897, ON A CALIFORNIA RANCH. JUDGE MILLER AND HIS FAMILY PROVIDED A SAFE HOME TO MANY ANIMALS: HORSES, CATTLE, SHEEP AND DOGS.

THE FINEST, MOST HANDSOME OF ALL THESE ANIMALS WAS A YOUNG DOG NAMED BUCK.
HE WAS A FAVORITE PET OF JUDGE MILLER'S TWO SONS, AND WENT EVERYWHERE WITH THEM.

THE BIG DOG'S DAYS WERE CAREFREE AND HAPPY, AND HE LOVED LIFE ON THE RANCH...

BUT THEN SOMETHING HAPPENED IN THE FAR NORTH THAT WOULD CHANGE EVERYTHING!
YUKON GAZETTE
GOLD DISCOVERED IN ALASKA!!
MINERS RUSH NORTH BIG SHORTAGE OF SLED DOGS!

ONE OF JUDGE MILLER'S FARMHANDS, A RATTY LITTLE MAN, WATCHED BUCK GREEDILY.
THAT'S A FINE DOG! BIG AND STRONG. WORTH A LOT OF MONEY!

AND SEVERAL DAYS LATER...
HO, BUCK, COME WITH ME. WE'LL GO FOR A NICE WALK IN THE WOODS. HUNT RACCOONS, EH?

TRUSTING AND INNOCENT, BUCK FOLLOWED THE MAN INTO THE WOODS.

SUDDENLY...

A NOOSE TIGHTENED AROUND BUCK'S NECK, AND HE LOST CONSCIOUSNESS.

$50?! FOR BUCK? THAT'S ALL I GET FOR SUCH A FINE DOG?
TAKE IT OR LEAVE IT, WEASEL.

BUCK'S CAGE WAS PILED ON A WAGON WITH MANY OTHERS.
A GOOD HAUL. NOW TO THE SHIP!

BY THE TIME BUCK CAME TO, HE WAS A PRISONER ON A RUSTY OLD TRAMP STEAMER BOUND FOR ALASKA! NOBODY PAID ANY ATTENTION TO THE DESPERATE HOWLS OF THE KIDNAPPED DOGS.
HHOOWW
OOOOOOOWW

NOTE TO READERS: THERE'S NO EXCUSE FOR BEING CRUEL TO AN ANIMAL. ANIMALS, JUST LIKE PEOPLE, LEARN BEST WHEN TRAINED GENTLY, FIRMLY AND RESPECTFULLY.

SOON BUCK LEARNED TO FEAR THE CLUB. HE STAYED WARY, ON GUARD...

...BUT AS HARD AS HE TRIED, THE CLUB STOPPED HIM AGAIN AND AGAIN.

THE CONTEST OF WILLS WENT ON FOR A LONG TIME:
140 POUNDS OF ANGRY DOG AGAINST A CRUEL MAN WITH A DANGEROUS CLUB!

AT LAST BUCK UNDERSTOOD: IF HE OBEYED, THE MAN WOULDN'T HURT HIM. THE BRAVE DOG WAS TIRED, BUT HIS FIGHTING SPIRIT WAS UNBROKEN.
THE BIG MAN SMILED AND PATTED HIM.
WELL, BUCK, MY BOY, YOU'VE LEARNED YOUR LESSON. NOW YOU KNOW YOUR PLACE, AND I KNOW MINE. YOU'LL BE A WONDERFUL SLED DOG.

ONE DAY SOON, BUCK HAD HIS CHANCE.
HE'S MY BEST DOG. I WANT AT LEAST $300 FOR HIM.
IT'S A DEAL.

THE TWO MEN WHO BOUGHT BUCK WERE GOING TO DELIVER MAIL AND SUPPLIES TO THE GOLD-MINING TOWN OF SKAGWAY.
HE'LL BE A GOOD WORKER, FRANÇOIS.
I HOPE YOU'RE RIGHT!

THEY PUT A LEATHER HARNESS ON BUCK, THEN LED HIM TO A SLED WHERE OTHER DOGS EYED HIM SUSPICIOUSLY-- ESPECIALLY SPITZ, THE BIG BLACK LEAD DOG.
GIVE HIM THE NUMBER FIVE SPOT, PERRAULT.

SOON THE MEN LOADED THEIR GEAR AND STARTED OFF ON THE TRAIL. BUCK WAS NOW PART OF THE SLED TEAM, HEADING INTO THE FROZEN WILDERNESS.
MUSH! MUSH! HO, SPITZ! RUN, CURLY! KEEP GOING, BUCK!

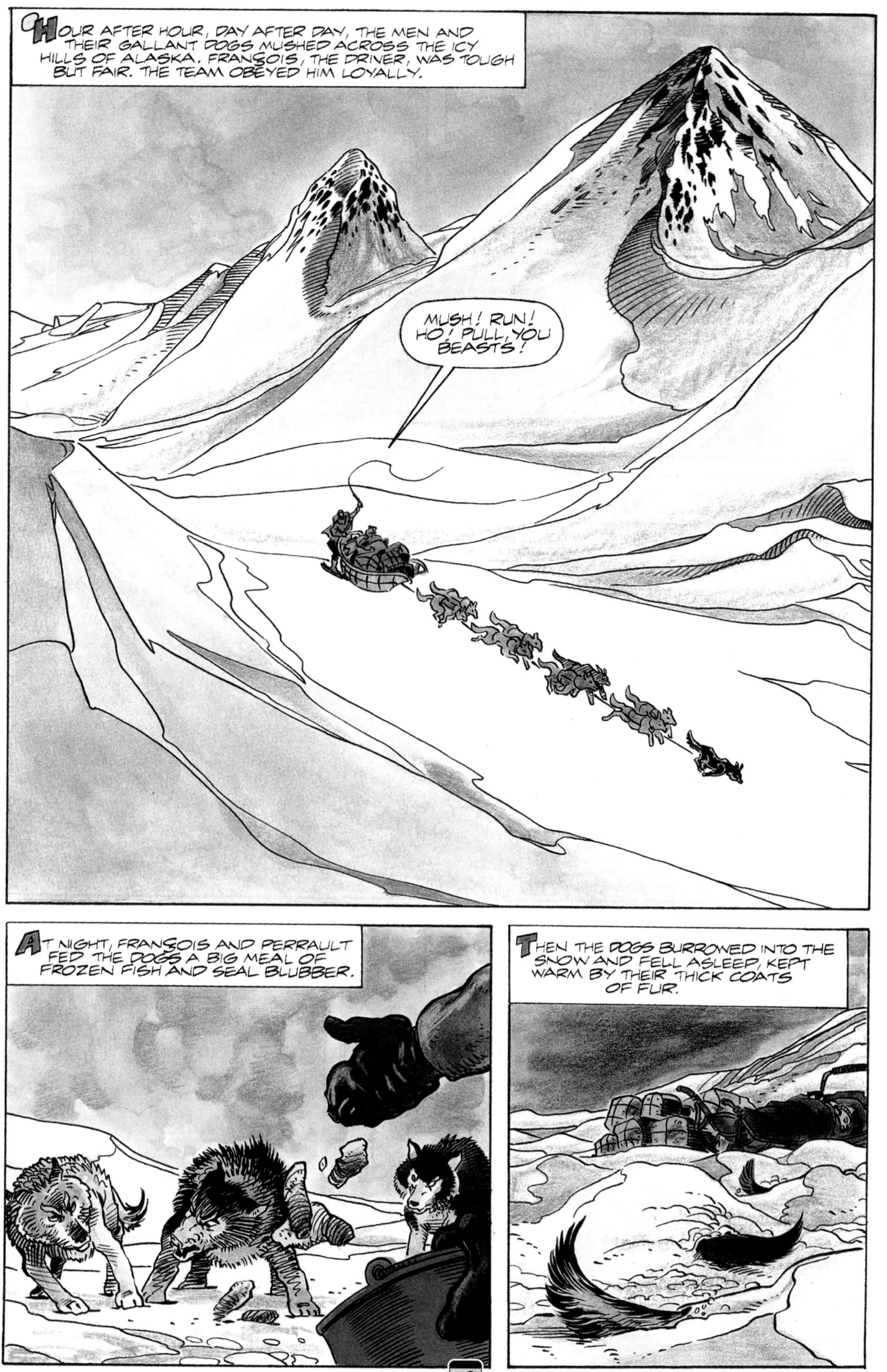

HOUR AFTER HOUR, DAY AFTER DAY, THE MEN AND THEIR GALLANT DOGS MUSHED ACROSS THE ICY HILLS OF ALASKA. FRANÇOIS, THE DRIVER, WAS TOUGH BUT FAIR. THE TEAM OBEYED HIM LOYALLY.

MUSH! RUN! HO! PULL, YOU BEASTS!

RACING TO THE GOLD FIELDS, THE TEAM CLIMBED HIGH, CRAGGY PEAKS...
MUSH!

...AND PLUNGED INTO DEEP, SNOW-FILLED VALLEYS.

WITH STAMINA AND COURAGE, THE BIG HUSKIES PUSHED THROUGH SUDDEN BLINDING SNOWSTORMS... BLIZZARDS SO THICK THEY COULD HARDLY FIND THEIR WAY!

IT WAS HARD WORK, BUT BUCK LOVED IT. HE QUICKLY LEARNED TO PULL HIS WEIGHT ON THE FAST-MOVING TEAM... AND TO STAY AWAY FROM THE MEAN, SLY SPITZ.

THAT BUCK-- SOME BEAST, EH?
WONDERFUL! OLD SPITZ IS GETTING JEALOUS!

THE ACTIVE LIFE OF THE TRAIL WAS GOOD FOR BUCK. HE GREW SMARTER AND STRONGER, AND HIS MUSCLES WERE LIKE STEEL.

AT LAST THE DAY CAME WHEN HE HAD A NEW DREAM:
HE WANTED TO BECOME LEADER OF THE PACK.

BUCK GREW TIRED OF THE WAY SPITZ BULLIED THE OTHER DOGS AND STOLE THEIR FOOD. ALL THE DOGS WERE AFRAID OF SPITZ--ALL EXCEPT BUCK, WHO EYED HIM WITH GROWING RAGE.
RRAWF!

THEN, ONE NIGHT IN CAMP, BUCK STEPPED IN. HE SNARLED A CHALLENGE... AND SPITZ ACCEPTED.
GR-RR.
ARRRG--

UH-OH. THIS IS BAD.
LET THEM FIGHT, PERRAULT. IT HAD TO COME SOONER OR LATER.

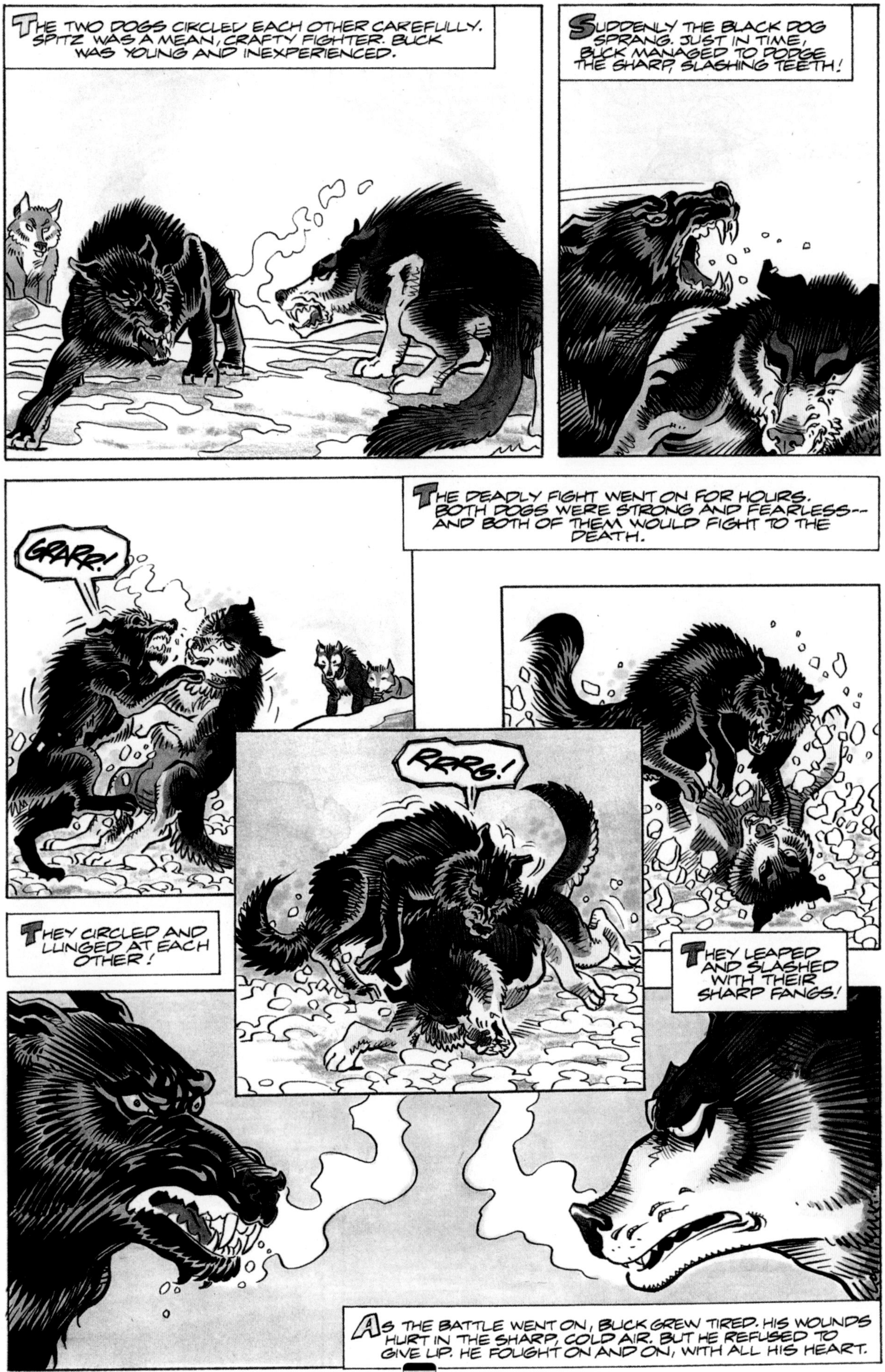

THE DEADLY FIGHT WENT ON FOR HOURS. BOTH DOGS WERE STRONG AND FEARLESS-- AND BOTH OF THEM WOULD FIGHT TO THE DEATH.

GRARR!

THEY CIRCLED AND LUNGED AT EACH OTHER!

RRRG!

THEY LEAPED AND SLASHED WITH THEIR SHARP FANGS!

AS THE BATTLE WENT ON, BUCK GREW TIRED. HIS WOUNDS HURT IN THE SHARP, COLD AIR. BUT HE REFUSED TO GIVE UP. HE FOUGHT ON AND ON, WITH ALL HIS HEART.

IN THE END, YOUTH AND COURAGE WON OUT. SPITZ THE BULLY WAS DEAD, AND BUCK WAS THE VICTOR.

NOW HE TOOK HIS PLACE AS THE RIGHTFUL LEADER OF THE PACK.
MUSH, LADS! GO, BUCK!

WITH BUCK IN CHARGE, THE TEAM FAIRLY FLEW ALONG THE TRAIL, AND BEFORE LONG--
WE MADE IT, FRANÇOIS!
SKAGWAY, AT LAST!

THE MEN HAD ORDERS TO REMAIN IN SKAGWAY, SO FOR THEM THE JOURNEY WAS OVER. BUT THEY WEREN'T HAPPY.
WE'LL HAVE TO SELL THE TEAM, PERRAULT.
I KNOW, AND I'M SURE GONNA MISS 'EM.

BUCK'S NEW OWNER WAS A VETERAN GOLD PROSPECTOR. JOHN THORNTON WAS A KINDLY MAN.
YOU AND I WILL GET TO BE GOOD FRIENDS, BUCK. WE NEED EACH OTHER.

THORNTON AND HIS PARTNERS WERE ON THE TRAIL OF A SECRET GOLD MINE DEEP IN YUKON TERRITORY.
ACCORDING TO THIS MAP, IT'S ABOUT FOUR MILES WEST OF DAWSON.
LET'S GET STARTED!

ONCE AGAIN, BUCK FOUND HIMSELF IN HARNESS, LEADING THE TEAM.
MUSH, LADS!
DAWSON

FOR MANY LONG COLD DAYS AND NIGHTS, THE PROSPECTORS FOUGHT THEIR WAY INTO THE WILDERNESS...

...AND FINALLY--
LOOK!
BY JINGO, WE FOUND IT!

THORNTON MADE SURE BUCK AND HIS TEAM HAD A HEARTY MEAL.
GOOD WORK, OLD FRIEND. YOU AND THE OTHERS EARNED YOUR REST!

BUCK BECAME DEVOTED TO JOHN THORNTON. HE LOVED HIS KIND OWNER WITH ALL HIS LOYAL HEART. HIS EYES FOLLOWED HIM EVERYWHERE.

EVERY DAY THE MEN WORKED HARD, DIGGING GOLD ORE FROM THE RICH MINE...

AT NIGHT THEY SAT PEACEFULLY AROUND THE CAMPFIRE WHILE THE DOGS RESTED NEARBY.

THEN, ONE MOONLIT NIGHT, BUCK HEARD STRANGE SOUNDS FLOATING FROM DEEP IN THE FOREST. HIS EARS PRICKED UP. THE MYSTERIOUS HOWLS STIRRED STRANGE YEARNINGS IN HIS HEART.

TIME AFTER TIME, THE BIG DOG HEARD THE WILD MYSTERIOUS CALL. EVERYTHING IN HIM WANTED TO FOLLOW... BUT HE COULDN'T LEAVE HIS BELOVED MASTER.
HOW'S MY FRIEND?
ROWF!

ONE MORNING, THE CALL CAME AGAIN. THIS TIME THE NEED TO FOLLOW WAS OVERPOWERING, AND BUCK SLIPPED OUT OF CAMP.

RACING OVER THE FROZEN WHITE HILLS, BUCK FOLLOWED THE CALL--A CALL THAT WAKENED ANCIENT MEMORIES BURIED DEEP INSIDE HIM.

FINALLY, HE KNEW WHAT THE SOUND WAS:
IT WAS A BAND OF WOLVES, PROWLING THROUGH THE FOREST!

FOR TWO DAYS, BUCK TRACKED THE WOLF PACK. HE WANTED TO RACE WITH THEM OVER THE FROZEN SNOW.

BUT THE PULL OF HIS OLD LIFE WON OUT. STILL YEARNING FOR JOHN THORNTON'S KIND VOICE, HE HEADED HOME.

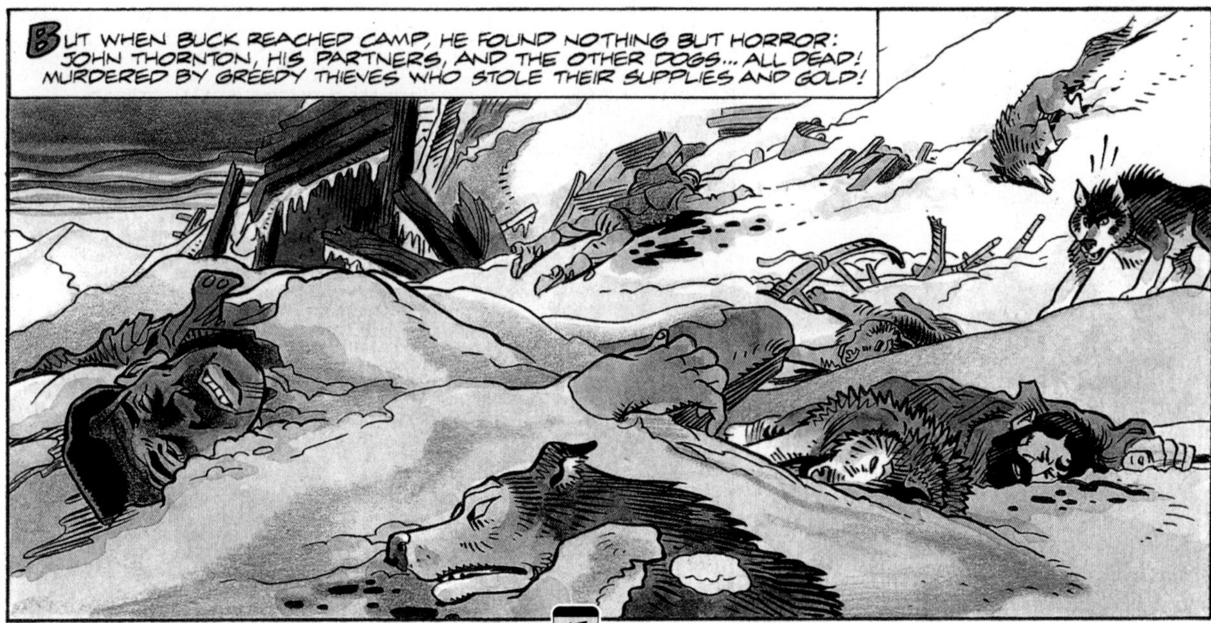
BUT WHEN BUCK REACHED CAMP, HE FOUND NOTHING BUT HORROR: JOHN THORNTON, HIS PARTNERS, AND THE OTHER DOGS... ALL DEAD! MURDERED BY GREEDY THIEVES WHO STOLE THEIR SUPPLIES AND GOLD!

BUCK HOVERED NEAR THE BODY OF HIS BELOVED MASTER, SICK WITH GRIEF. HIS STRONG BODY SHIVERED WITH PAIN.

THEN HIS GRIEF TURNED TO RAGE. HE WOULD FIND THE KILLERS! HE WOULD TRACK THEM DOWN AND REAP REVENGE!

NOSE TO THE GROUND, GROWLING WITH FURY, THE BIG DOG PICKED UP THE SCENT OF THE EVILDOERS.

STUBBORNLY HE FOLLOWED THEIR TRAIL ALL DAY, WITHOUT STOPPING TO REST OR HUNT FOR FOOD...

...AND AS EVENING DREW NEAR, BUCK TRACKED DOWN THE GUILTY BAND OF SAVAGE OUTLAWS. HE WATCHED WITH RAGE AS THEY USED SUPPLIES FROM JOHN THORNTON... SUPPLIES THAT STILL BORE THE KIND MAN'S SCENT.
JT

THEN BUCK HOWLED WITH RAGE! HIS EYES BLAZED RED! REVENGE! *REVENGE!*
RAARRGH!

CAUGHT BY SURPRISE, THE MEN HAD NEVER KNOWN SUCH FURY! SLASHING CLAWS AND FANGS, BUCK EXPLODED AMONG THEM LIKE A HURRICANE, A TORNADO, A THUNDERBOLT!
AARRGH!

THE ATTACK WAS FAST BUT DEADLY. A FEW OF THE VILLAINS ESCAPED, BUT NOT MANY. BUCK WAS SATISFIED. HE HAD AVENGED HIS MASTER. JUSTICE HAD BEEN DONE.

AS RAGE FADED, GRIEF FLOODED BACK. BUCK THREW HIS HEAD UP AND WAILED TO THE SKY. HIS ONLY FRIEND WAS GONE.
OOOOOWHOOOWW!

THEN HE TURNED HIS BACK FOREVER ON THE WORLD OF MEN, AND HEADED NORTH TO FIND THE WOLVES...

...AND FOREVER AFTER, THE MEN OF THE FROZEN NORTH SHIVERED WHEN THEY TOLD OF A WILD GHOST DOG WHO STILL RUNS AT THE HEAD OF THE PACK-- A HUGE, FEARLESS ANIMAL...ONCE A GENTLE PET... WHO FINALLY ANSWERED...
THE END
THE CALL OF THE WILD.

JACK LONDON

JACK LONDON WAS ONE OF THE BEST PAID AND MOST POPULAR AUTHORS OF HIS TIME. LONDON WAS BORN JOHN GRIFFITH CHANEY ON JANUARY 12, 1876, IN SAN FRANCISCO, CALIFORNIA. HIS FATHER LEFT HIS MOTHER BEFORE JACK WAS BORN, AND SHE MARRIED JOHN LONDON WHEN JACK WAS JUST EIGHT MONTHS OLD. JACK LEFT SCHOOL AFTER EIGHTH GRADE, BUT HE LOVED READING AND SPENT MUCH TIME AT THE LIBRARY, EDUCATING HIMSELF. HE WOULD LATER RETURN TO FINISH HIGH SCHOOL, WHILE WORKING AS A JANITOR. AFTER LEAVING SCHOOL, LONDON TRAVELED THROUGHOUT THE UNITED STATES AND ABROAD AND WORKED A VARIETY OF JOBS, INCLUDING JOBS AS A SAILOR, FACTORY WORKER, AND GOLD PROSPECTOR. AT ONE POINT, HE TRAVELED AS A HOBO, OR "TRAMP," ON TRAINS. LONDON USED HIS MANY EXPERIENCES IN HIS WRITING. HE WAS ALSO ACTIVE POLITICALLY—HE RAN FOR OFFICE TWICE BUT LOST BOTH TIMES. LONDON BEGAN WRITING SHORT STORIES IN THE 1890S AND PUBLISHED A COLLECTION OF THEM, CALLED **THE SON OF THE WOLF**, IN 1900. IN 1902, HE PUBLISHED HIS FIRST NOVEL, **THE DAUGHTER OF THE SNOWS**. JUST A YEAR LATER, HE PUBLISHED **THE CALL OF THE WILD**, A BOOK THAT EARNED HIM WORLDWIDE RECOGNITION AS A WRITER. AFTER HIS WRITING CAREER WAS LAUNCHED, HE CONTINUED

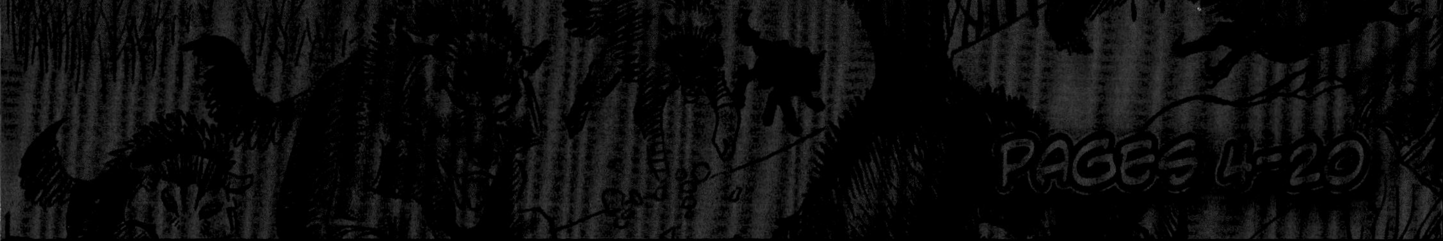

PAGES 4-20

HENRY FLEMING WAS A YOUNG FARM BOY WHO ENLISTED IN THE 304th NEW YORK VOLUNTEERS AND MARCHED OFF TO WAR WITH HIS GOOD FRIEND, JIM CONKLIN.

MY FIRST BATTLE! AM I THE ONLY ONE OUT HERE WHO'S SCARED TO DEATH? AM-AM I BRAVE ENOUGH TO FIGHT? OR WILL I RUN LIKE A RABBIT?

HERE THEY COME!

PAGES 22-38

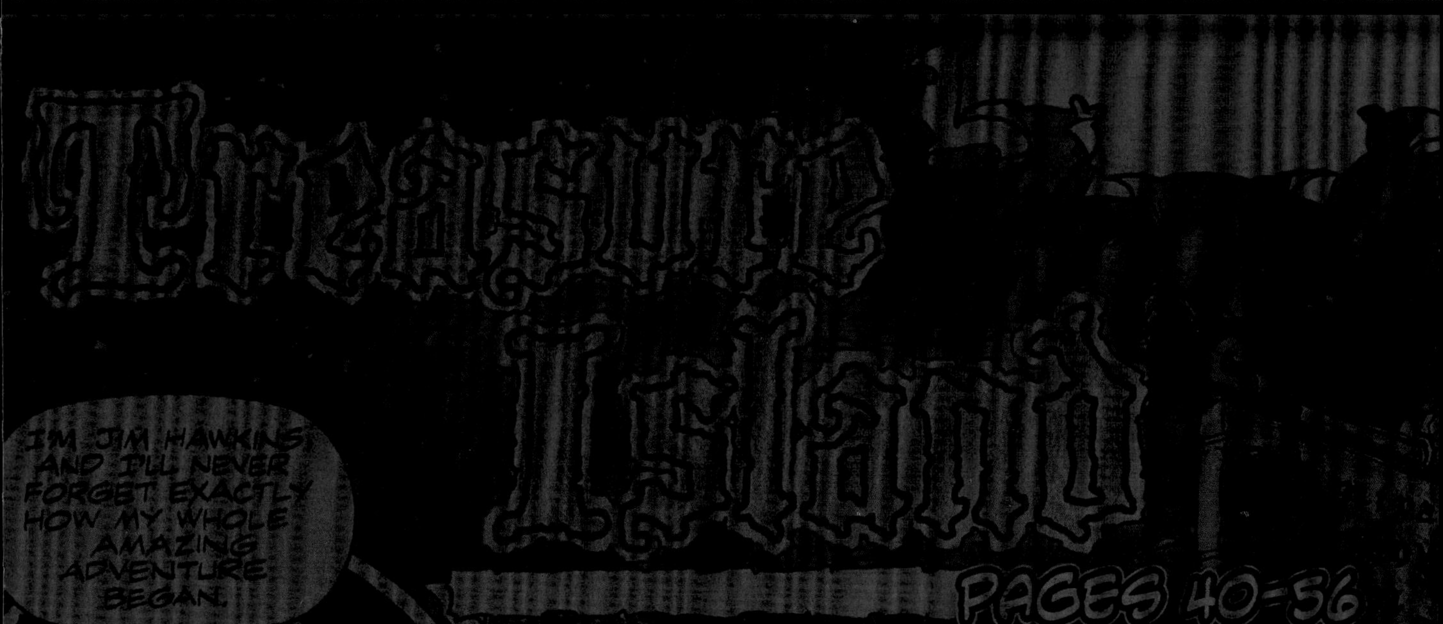

[Treasure Island]

I'M JIM HAWKINS AND I'LL NEVER FORGET EXACTLY HOW MY WHOLE AMAZING ADVENTURE BEGAN.

PAGES 40-56

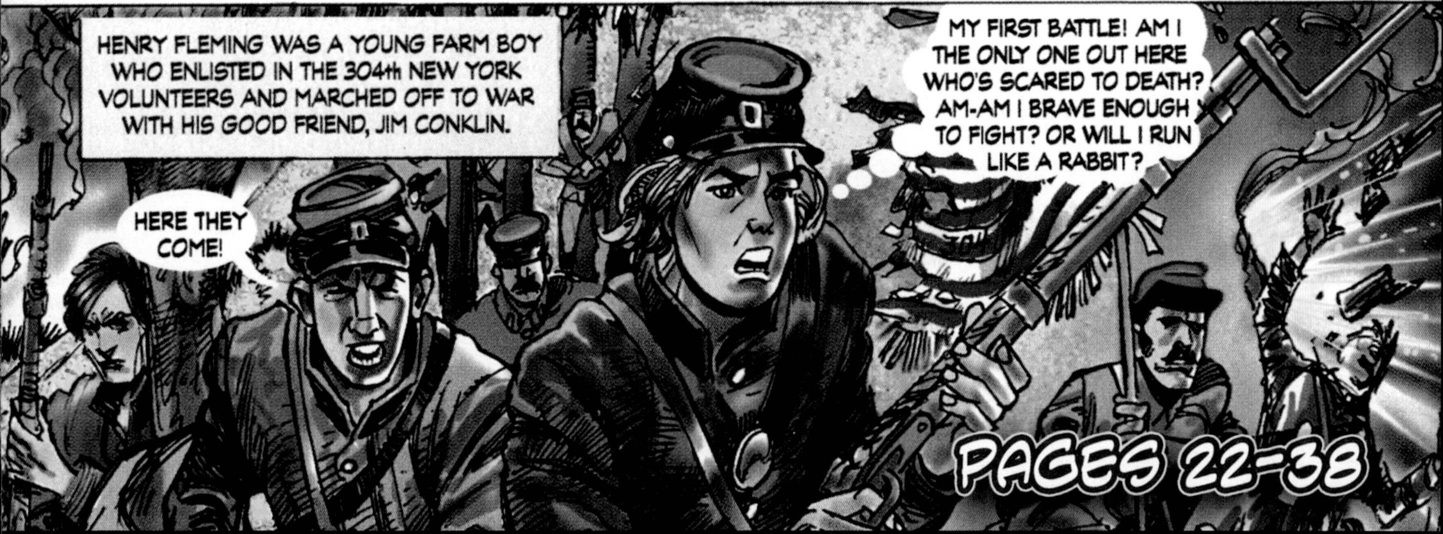

THE RED BADGE OF COURAGE

by STEPHEN CRANE

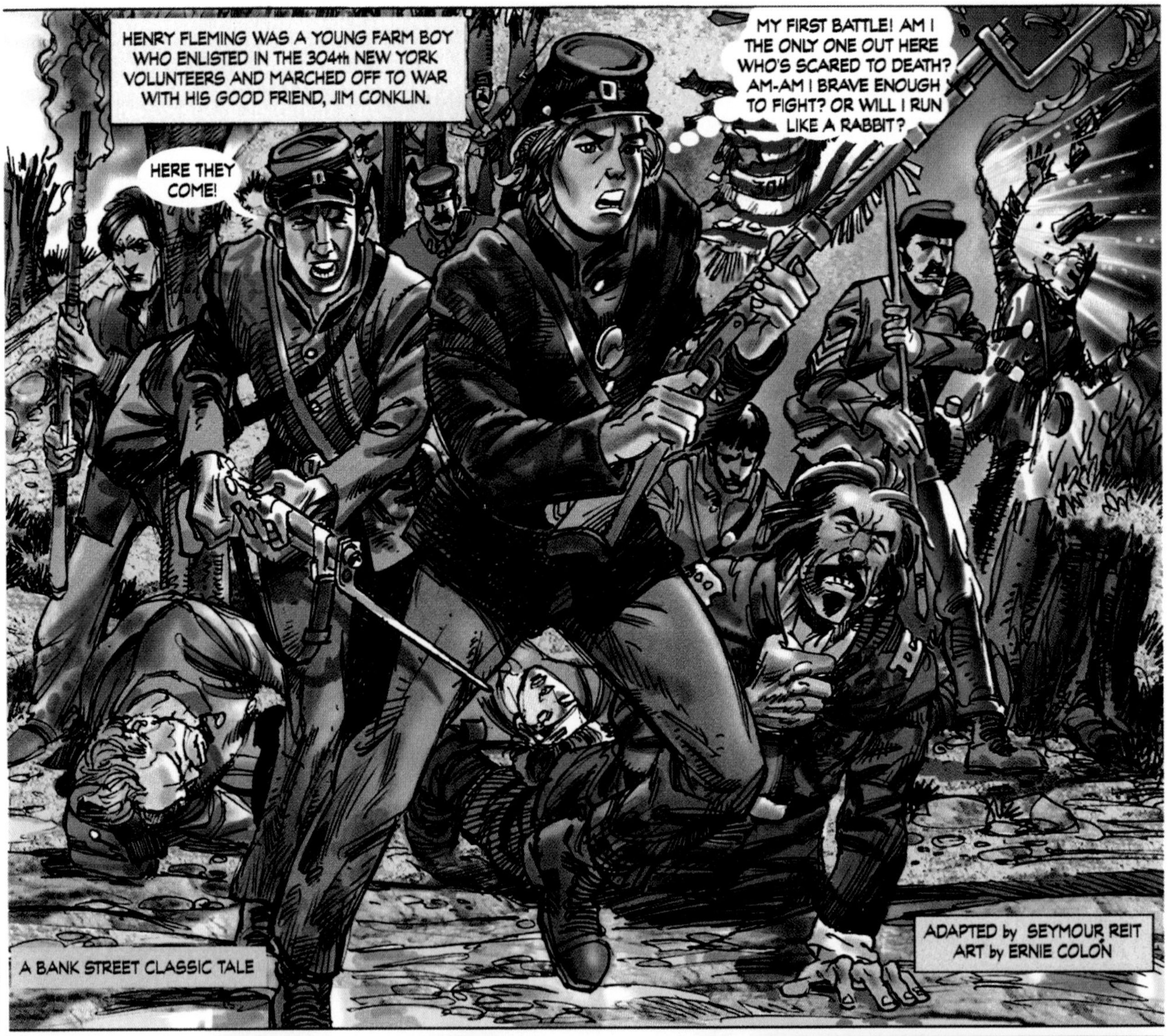

HENRY FLEMING WAS A YOUNG FARM BOY WHO ENLISTED IN THE 304th NEW YORK VOLUNTEERS AND MARCHED OFF TO WAR WITH HIS GOOD FRIEND, JIM CONKLIN.

MY FIRST BATTLE! AM I THE ONLY ONE OUT HERE WHO'S SCARED TO DEATH? AM-AM I BRAVE ENOUGH TO FIGHT? OR WILL I RUN LIKE A RABBIT?

HERE THEY COME!

A BANK STREET CLASSIC TALE

ADAPTED by SEYMOUR REIT
ART by ERNIE COLON

TO LIVE HONORABLY, ALL OF US MUST COME TO TERMS WITH OUR OWN FEARS...AND DISCOVER OUR OWN COURAGE. THIS IS THE STORY OF ONE YOUNG MAN'S SEARCH FOR COURAGE AND DIGNITY AMIDST THE CHAOS AND TERROR OF AMERICA'S CIVIL WAR.

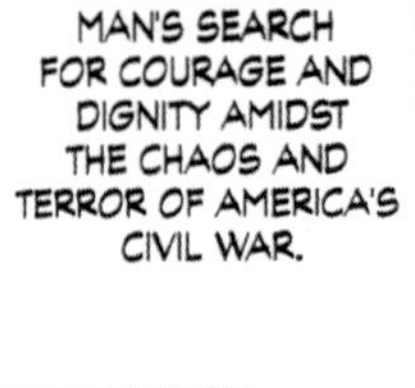

LATER THAT NIGHT, THE WEARY REGIMENT MADE CAMP ON THE BANKS OF A WIDE RIVER.
AWRR-- ME POOR ACHIN' FEET!
WISH WE HAD SOMETHING DECENT TO EAT BESIDES HARDTACK.
TASTES LIKE OLD SAWDUST.
US
THE REBS LOOK SO CLOSE, JIM.
JEST WAIT, HENRY. SOON YOU'LL SEE ONE OF THE BIGGEST BATTLES EVER WAS.
I HEARD A RUMOR--WE'RE A-GOIN' TO CROSS THAT RIVER TOMORROW AND HIT THEM FROM THE REAR.
HAW--YOU AND YOUR RUMORS, WILSON. NOTHIN' BUT HOGWASH.
FOR ONCE, WILSON'S RUMOR PROVED TO BE RIGHT.
304th REGIMENT! FORM COLUMNS OF FOUR! LIGHT GEAR ONLY! FALL IN QUICKLY, MEN!
MARCHING BRISKLY, THE TROOPS CROSSED THE RIVER ON A HASTILY BUILT PONTOON BRIDGE. HENRY FELT PANIC CLUTCH HIM LIKE AN ICY HAND.

THE MEN REACHED A FOREST AND FORMED A SKIRMISH LINE. ENEMY BULLETS BEGAN SNAPPING THROUGH THE TREES.
WE'RE IN FOR IT NOW!
WHACK!
I TOLD YOU!
C-CAN I DO IT?
TO HENRY, THE REBEL BULLETS SOUNDED LIKE ENRAGED HORNETS. THEN THE REBEL CANNONS BOOMED THEIR LOUD VOICES.

BOOM!

THE LINE BROKE INTO FRAGMENTS. THE MEN MOVED FORWARD, CROUCHING. NOW, AT LAST, THEY FACED WAR--THE FIERCE RED ANIMAL, THE BLOOD-SWOLLEN TIDE.

THE ATTACK SOON FALTERED. THE MEN TOOK REFUGE IN A NEARBY DITCH AND HID BEHIND ANYTHING THEY COULD FIND.
STAY DOWN, HENRY!

WHY DON'T THEY SEND IN HELP?

THE REBS ARE TOUGH FIGHTERS.
THEY WERE SUPPOSED TO RUN AS SOON AS THEY SAW US. GUESS WE WERE WRONG, HUH?
STEADY FIRE FROM THE REBEL CANNONS KEPT THE REGIMENT PINNED DOWN.
HASBROUCK, MOVE YOUR BOYS OFF TO THE RIGHT! THE REBS ARE STARTING A FLANK ATTACK!
YES, SIR!

THE MEN JUMPED TO THEIR FEET AND TRIED TO MOVE FORWARD AS ENEMY FIRE WHISTLED EVERYWHERE AROUND THEM.

BUT NOT EVERYONE ADVANCED.
WHAT'S HAPPENING, JIM?
BEATS ME! THEY SAY SOME OF OUR BOYS ARE RUNNING OFF--

HENRY WATCHED IN TERROR AS THE CONFEDERATE TROOPS SURGED FORWARD WITH A BLOODCURDLING REBEL YELL.
WHY-- IT-- IT LOOKS LIKE THERE'S ABOUT A MILLION OF 'EM!
BLAM!
THE BATTLE SURGED BACK AND FORTH TILL THE MEN ON BOTH SIDES COULD BARELY SEE OR BREATHE IN THE HEAT, NOISE AND SMOKE. HENRY, IN A KIND OF "BATTLE SLEEP," MOVED FORWARD BLINDLY--PART OF THE TORN, BLEEDING BODY OF HIS BRIGADE.

KEEP GOING! DON'T STOP! I'LL SHOOT THE FIRST MAN WHO HOLDS BACK!

WE NEED SUPPORT! WE NEED SUPPORT!
WHERE'S THE GENERAL? WHERE'S OUR SUPPORT?

ZING!

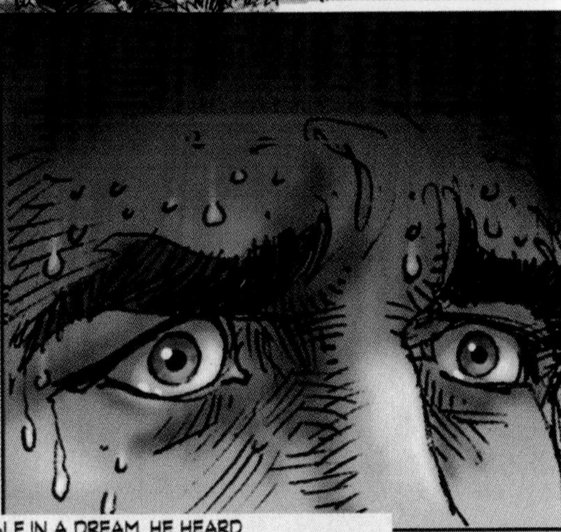

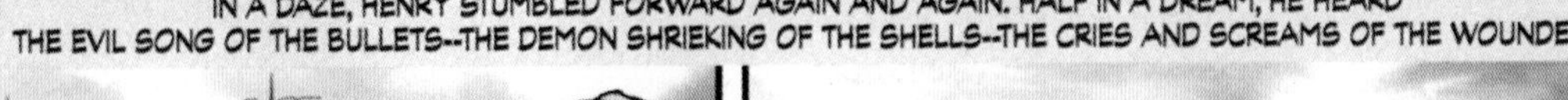
IN A DAZE, HENRY STUMBLED FORWARD AGAIN AND AGAIN. HALF IN A DREAM, HE HEARD THE EVIL SONG OF THE BULLETS--THE DEMON SHRIEKING OF THE SHELLS--THE CRIES AND SCREAMS OF THE WOUNDED!

HENRY FLEMING TURNED AND RAN BLINDLY AWAY FROM THE BATTLE, HIS BODY QUIVERING, HIS KNEES READY TO BUCKLE. EVERYTHING WAS A BLUR. THE AIR HE BREATHED FELT HOT WITH BULLETS AND BLOOD.
OOOF!
GASP... GASP...
HENRY TORE THROUGH THE WOODS TILL HE REACHED A DIRT ROAD AND DROPPED WITH EXHAUSTION.
PANT... COUGH...
I HAD TO--I HAD TO. IT WAS NORMAL TO SAVE MY OWN LIFE. N-NOT COWARDLY...OTHERS RAN TOO.
NATURE WAS ALIVE ALL AROUND HENRY. HE THREW A PINECONE AT A PLAYFUL SQUIRREL.
SEE? EVEN THAT SQUIRREL PROTECTS ITSELF. IT'S NATURAL TO RUN AS FAST AS YOU CAN FROM DANGER.

HENRY FLED DEEP INTO THE WOODS, AWAY FROM THE RUMBLE OF BATTLE. HE WAS AMAZED TO SEE A PURE BLUE SKY AND THE SUN GLEAMING ON TREES AND FIELDS.

BUT HENRY FELT NO PEACE. HE DREADED THE SCORN OF HIS BRAVER COMRADES, AND PEERED CAUTIOUSLY FROM BEHIND COVER AT HIS BATTALION HEADQUARTERS.
GENERAL! GENERAL, SIR! OUR BOYS STOPPED THE REBS!

THEY'RE FALLING BACK, SIR-- ALL ALONG THE LINE!
WE HELD 'EM, BY GEORGE! WE HELD 'EM! THANK HEAVENS!

SUDDENLY, HENRY FELT SICK AT HEART.
OUR MEN HELD--AND I--I RAN AWAY. I FAILED THEM. I'M JUST--A C-COWARD!

DEEPLY ASHAMED AND WANDERING AIMLESSLY, HENRY SPOTTED A SOLDIER SITTING VERY QUIETLY UNDER A TREE.
WHO'S THAT, SITTING THERE? MAYBE A-- DESERTER--LIKE ME.
OOOH, NO!
THE DEAD MAN AND THE LIVING MAN EXCHANGED A LONG LOOK. HORROR-STRUCK, HENRY BACKED AWAY FROM THE "THING" THAT ONCE WAS A MAN.
HENRY STUMBLED AWAY WITH A STRANGE FEAR THAT THE CORPSE MIGHT SPRING UP AND PURSUE HIM. HE HEARD THE CRIMSON ROAR OF BATTLE AGAIN AS HE STUMBLED INTO A GROUP OF WOUNDED UNION SOLDIERS TRUDGING AWAY FROM BATTLE.
THAT WERE A PRETTY GOOD FIGHT, WEREN'T IT?
ER--UH--

WHERE YOU WOUNDED, LAD?
WHAT?! ME? OH--I--THAT IS, ER--

WHERE YOU HIT?

FILLED WITH SHAME, HENRY SLID THROUGH THE CROWD AND FADED INTO THE MARCHING STREAM.
HEY--WHERE YOU GOIN', LAD?

SUDDENLY--
WH--! JIM! JIM CONKLIN!
HELLO, HENRY.

WHAT HAPPENED, JIM?
WELL, NOW--I WAS OUT THERE. GOOD FIGHT, HENRY. THEN I--GOT HIT--COUPLE OF PLACES. YES, B'JIMINEY, I GOT SHOT.

CLEAR THE ROAD, MEN! ARTILLERY'S COMIN' THROUGH!

WATCH IT, LADS!
HEY!
LOOK LIVELY!
THIS WAY, JIM--QUICK!
OOOH--I'M-- COUGH--
EASY WE GO, MATE. YOU'LL BE ALL RIGHT SOON. YOU WILL! I'LL--
JIM!!?
HE'S DEAD--DEAD-- MY FRIEND JIM CONKLIN! IT'S--NOT RIGHT. N-NOT RIGHT!

AFTER JIM'S HASTY BURIAL, HENRY AND THE WOUNDED MEN SLOWLY APPROACHED THE BATTLE'S FURNACE ROAR. SUDDENLY, A FEW UNION SOLDIERS CRASHED TOWARD THEM.
THEY--THEY'RE ALL RUNNING--RETREATING. MAYBE... MAYBE I'M NOT SUCH A COWARD AFTER ALL.
IN QUICK RETREAT FROM THE STORMING ENEMY, WILD-EYED UNION TROOPS SWEPT OUT OF THE WOODS AND PAST THE RAGTAG CLUMP OF WOUNDED SOLDIERS.

WHY--WHAT'RE YOU DOING? WHERE YOU GOING?
LEMME GO! LEMME GO!
AHHH...

YEH SEEM TO BE IN A BAD WAY, BOY. HERE-- LET ME HELP YOU.

YEH'RE FROM THE 304th?
BY JINGO, I BELIEVE THEY'RE CAMPED JUST YONDER. SEE THEIR FIRE? COME ALONG--I'LL TAKE YOU THERE, BOY.

HENRY LIMPED UNSTEADILY TOWARD THE FIRE, FEARING THE GREETING HIS OLD COMRADES WOULD GIVE HIM.
HEY, LOOKEE-- IT'S FLEMING!
BY GOLLY!
WELCOME BACK, HENRY!

HE'S WOUNDED!
LOOKS LIKE HE TOOK A SHOT TO HIS HEAD. MUST HURT LIKE THUNDER. LET'S GET YOU CLEANED UP, LAD.

BY GINGER, I'M GLAD TO SEE YEH.
I THOUGHT YEH WAS DEAD SURE ENOUGH. HALF OUR MEN GOT SEPARATED IN ALL THAT MESS--WANDERED AROUND LOST, JUST LIKE YOU.

IT--FEELS RIGHT GOOD TO BE BACK, WILSON.
'COURSE IT DOES. NOW GET Y'SELF SOME SLEEP. YOU CAN USE MY BLANKETS.
HENRY FLEMING SUDDENLY FELT BLESSED. NOBODY SUSPECTED HIS COWARDICE. HIS GUILTY SECRET WAS SAFE. THE GROUND FELT LIKE THE SOFTEST COUCH.

HENRY WANTED TO SLEEP FOR A THOUSAND YEARS. BUT THE GRAY MISTS OF MORNING CAME ALL TOO SOON.

THE NOISE OF GUNFIRE STILL SPLINTERED AND BLARED IN THE DISTANCE.
HARD TO BELIEVE A MAN CAN CHANGE SO MUCH IN ONE DAY...I DON'T CARE ONE SPECK ABOUT BEING A HIGH-FALUTIN' HERO ANYMORE. I JUST WANT TO--WELL, DO MY DUTY AS A SOLDIER.
I KNOW.

HENRY'S RAGGED REGIMENT MARCHED TOWARD THE TRENCHES THROUGH THE BOOM AND CRACKLE OF GUNFIRE. HENRY FELT LIKE A MAN REBORN--A MAN WITH A SECOND CHANCE TO PROVE HIS METTLE.
THINK WE'RE HEADED INTO ANOTHER SCRAP?
YEP. THAT'S HOW I HEARD IT.
AT MIDDAY, HENRY'S REGIMENT STRUGGLED UP A HIGH RIDGE TO RELIEVE SOME WORN-OUT TROOPS WHO HAD HELD THE LINE ALL NIGHT. HE COULD HEAR CANNON FIRE JUST AHEAD.
WILL I PANIC AGAIN?
PEERING OVER THE RIDGE, HENRY SAW THE JOHNNY REBS IN THEIR GRAY UNIFORMS. HIS HEART FILLED WITH RAGE AS HE THOUGHT OF JIM CONKLIN.
THIS TIME I'LL FIGHT TO THE END!
THE ORDER TO ATTACK CAME RACING DOWN THE LINE: "GO AT THEM, BOYS!" HENRY AND HIS COMRADES SURGED FORWARD-- INTO A GRIM HAIL OF ENEMY BULLETS!
I'VE BEEN OUT AMONG THESE DRAGONS BEFORE-- BUT MAYBE THEY'RE NOT AS FEARSOME AS I THOUGHT.

BLAM!
BAM!
THE FIGHTING RAGED FOR HOURS. FALLING BACK, THE REBELS GATHERED BEHIND A LONG WOODEN FENCE.
HENRY FOUGHT LIKE A WILDCAT. HE FIRED TILL HIS RIFLE BURNED HIS HANDS. BUT HE WAS FILLED WITH A STRANGE, CALM CONFIDENCE. THERE WAS NO ROOM NOW FOR FEAR.
BLAM!
TO HIS SURPRISE, HE FOUND HIMSELF OUT IN FRONT OF THE ATTACK.
LIGHT-FOOTED, VERY MUCH ALIVE, HENRY SAW EVERYTHING WITH GREAT CLARITY--EVERY TREE, BUSH, BLADE OF GRASS. HE HEARD WITHOUT FEAR THE SONG OF THE BULLETS--WHICH SEEMED TO ARRIVE ON SCHEDULE, AS IF DELIVERED BY SOME VAST MACHINE.
UNH-HH--
JUST AS THE FLAG-BEARER WENT DOWN, HENRY GRABBED THE FLAG AND CHARGED FORWARD.
COME ON, LADS! THEY'RE ON THE RUN!

IN A FINAL DASH, WITH HENRY AT THE FORE, THE BRIGADE OVERRAN THE REBEL POSITION. MOST OF THE DEFENDERS FLED; A FEW WERE CAPTURED. THE MEN IN HENRY'S REGIMENT STOOD UP AND DANCED FOR JOY.

WE DID IT! WE LICKED 'EM! IF I HAD 10,000 WILDCATS LIKE YOU, HENRY, I COULD TEAR THE STOMACH OUT OF THIS WAR IN LESS THAN A WEEK!
EXCELLENT! YOUR MEN ALL DESERVE TO BE MAJOR-GENERALS!
THANK YOU, SIR!

HENRY FLEMING EMERGED FROM BATTLE WITH A NEW STORE OF STRONG AND STURDY BLOOD. HE HAD TOUCHED THE GREAT DEATH AND HAD NOT FLINCHED OR COWERED. FOR THE FIRST TIME, HE WAS IN TOUCH WITH HIS OWN MANHOOD--NEITHER TOO PROUD OF HIS COURAGE, NOR TOO ASHAMED OF HIS FEAR.
THE END

STEPHEN CRANE

STEPHEN CRANE'S **THE RED BADGE OF COURAGE** IS OFTEN BELIEVED TO BE THE FIRST AMERICAN WAR NOVEL. CRANE WAS BORN ON NOVEMBER 1, 1871, IN NEWARK, NEW JERSEY. HE WAS ONE OF FOURTEEN CHILDREN. CRANE BEGAN WRITING AT A YOUNG AGE. AT AGE EIGHT, HE STARTED WRITING SHORT STORIES, AND BY AGE SIXTEEN, HE WAS WRITING ARTICLES FOR THE **NEW YORK TRIBUNE**, A NEWSPAPER. THREE YEARS LATER, CRANE'S MOTHER DIED, AND HE LEFT HIS FAMILY HOME TO MOVE TO NEW YORK CITY. THERE, HE LIVED IN THE POOR PARTS OF THE CITY, WHILE HE WORKED AS A WRITER AND JOURNALIST. HE PUBLISHED HIS FIRST NOVEL, **MAGGIE: A GIRL OF THE STREETS**, IN 1893. THIS WORK BROUGHT TO LIFE THE FATE OF THE POOR IN NEW YORK CITY. MANY PEOPLE WERE NOT USED TO READING SUCH REALISTIC DESCRIPTIONS OF POVERTY, AND PUBLISHERS DID NOT WANT TO PRINT IT. CRANE HAD TO BORROW MONEY TO PUBLISH THE BOOK HIMSELF. IN 1895, HE PUBLISHED A BOOK OF POEMS AS WELL AS **THE RED BADGE OF COURAGE**. CRANE HAD YET TO SEE ANY ACTUAL BATTLES WHEN HE WROTE THE NOVEL, BUT HE BECAME INTERESTED IN REPORTING ON WARS FOR NEWSPAPERS AFTER HE PUBLISHED IT. THE NOVEL WAS A GREAT SUCCESS, AND MANY PEOPLE THOUGHT IT WAS WRITTEN BY A REAL SOLDIER. CRANE THEN TRAVELED TO CUBA, MEXICO, AND TEXAS TO COVER WARS. HE MOVED TO ENGLAND IN 1898 AND LEFT ENGLAND FOR CUBA TO COVER THE SPANISH-AMERICAN WAR IN 1899. CRANE, HOWEVER, GREW SICK IN CUBA AND RETURNED TO EUROPE. HE DIED IN 1900, WHEN HE WAS JUST 29 YEARS OLD. TWO MORE OF HIS WORKS WERE PUBLISHED AFTER HIS DEATH—**WOUNDS IN THE RAIN** AND **WHILOMVILLE STORIES**.

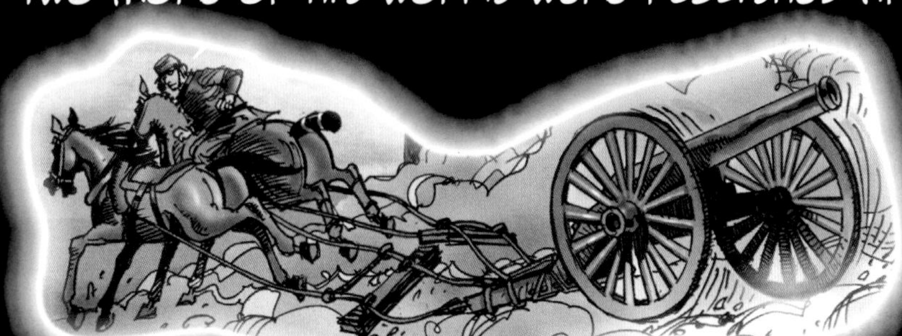

HERE THEY COME!

PAGES 22-38

Treasure Island

I'M JIM HAWKINS, AND I'LL NEVER FORGET EXACTLY HOW MY WHOLE AMAZING ADVENTURE BEGAN.

PAGES 40-56

ONE DARK NIGHT,

A BANK STREET CLASSIC TALE
ADAPTED BY SEYMOUR REIT
ART - ERNIE COLÓN
LETTERING - GEORGE ROBERTS
COLORS - LUISA COLÓN
Treasure Island
BY ROBERT LOUIS STEVENSON
Admiral Benbow Inn
I'M JIM HAWKINS, AND I'LL NEVER FORGET EXACTLY HOW MY WHOLE AMAZING ADVENTURE BEGAN.
ONE DARK NIGHT, A STRANGE SEAFARER POUNDED ON OUR INN DOOR...
BAM!
BAM!
AHOY, THERE! I NEED A ROOM! OPEN UP AND BE QUICK ABOUT IT!

THE SEAMAN HAD A DANGEROUS AIR ABOUT HIM, BUT MOTHER SHOWED HIM TO A GOOD ROOM.
PEACEFUL AND QUIET. JUST THE THING. I'LL *TAKE* IT.
VERY WELL, MR.--MR.--
JUST CALL ME BILLY BONES, MA'AM.

JUST AS I WAS ABOUT TO LEAVE, THE BUCCANEER PLUCKED MY SLEEVE...
HSST, LAD! I'LL GIVE YOU A SILVER COIN EVERY MONTH IF YOU WATCH FOR A SEAFARING MAN WITH A MISSING LEG.
AGREED?
ER--YES, SIR.

THE GRIZZLED OLD SEA DOG SEEMED FEARFUL OF SOMETHING. EVERY DAY HE PACED THE BEACH, STARING OUT TO SEA...

...AND EVERY NIGHT HE SWILLED LIQUOR, GETTING DRUNK AND FRIGHTENING THE OTHER GUESTS.
FIFTEEN MEN ON THE DEAD MAN'S CHEST! YO-HO-HO AND A BOTTLE OF RUM!

MONTHS WENT BY. BILLY BONES NEVER PAID US FOR HIS ROOM AND BOARD. ONE DAY HE HAD A VISITOR, A NASTY FELLOW LIKE HIMSELF.
BLACK DOG'S THE NAME. I'M LOOKING FOR A SAILOR CALLED BILLY BONES.
ER--YOU'LL FIND HIM IN THE PARLOR.

I HEARD THE MEN ARGUING. THEN BLACK DOG RACED OUT, CLUTCHING HIS BLOODY SHOULDER.
...AND DON'T EVER COME BACK AGAIN!

A WEEK LATER, A BLIND SAILOR FOUND HIS WAY TO OUR INN.
BILLY BONES IS IN HERE, SIR.
THANKEE, BOY.
BLIND PEW!
TAP
TAP
TAP

AYE, IT'S OLD BLIND PEW, MATE! THE LADS AND I HAVE A LITTLE MESSAGE FOR YOU! HEH, HEH!
OH, NO! NO!

AS THE BLIND MAN TAPPED HIS WAY OUT, BONES OPENED THE SLIP OF PAPER WITH TREMBLING FINGERS.
THE B-BLACK SPOT! IT M-MEANS DEATH!

BONES TURNED WHITE AS A SHEET.
JIM, YOU MUST HELP ME! THOSE CUTTHROATS WILL BE BACK ANY MINUTE!

MY TREASURE IS WORTH MILLIONS! I MUST ESCAPE BEFORE...
URGH-H!

HE GAVE A STRANGLED CRY AND FELL TO THE FLOOR.
GOOD HEAVENS-- THE MAN'S DEAD!

I RAN TO TELL MOTHER.
SHALL I SEND FOR DR. LIVESEY?
YES! BUT FIRST, LET'S GET THE MONEY THAT RASCAL OWES US!

WE MANAGED TO FIND THE KEY TO THE OLD SEA CHEST. WE HAULED IT OUT AND OPENED IT UP.
THERE MUST BE MONEY HIDDEN IN HERE SOMEWHERE.

MOTHER, HURRY! THOSE BRIGANDS MUST BE ON THEIR WAY!
I WILL! I ONLY WANT WHAT'S OURS-- NO MORE, NO LESS.

AS SHE COUNTED OUT GOLD PIECES, I HEARD A TAP-TAPPING IN THE DISTANCE. I PEERED FROM THE WINDOW--
UH-OH! HERE THEY COME! I CAN SEE BLIND PEW!

THEY'RE ALMOST HERE! HURRY, MOTHER! WE MUST RUN FOR OUR LIVES!

THERE WAS A PACKET WRAPPED IN OILSKIN AT THE VERY BOTTOM OF THE TRUNK.

RUN, MOTHER! I'LL TAKE THIS TO MAKE THINGS EVEN!

IT WAS A CLOSE CALL! AS THE BUCCANEERS RUSHED IN THE FRONT DOOR, WE SLIPPED OUT THE BACK WAY AND HEADED FOR THE NEARBY TOWN OF BRISTOL.
SSH! NOT A SOUND!

WE RAN ALL THE WAY TO THE HOUSE OF SQUIRE TRELAWNEY, THE MOST IMPORTANT MAN IN TOWN.

THE SQUIRE LISTENED TO OUR STORY WITH GREAT INTEREST.
BY GEORGE, YOU WERE LUCKY TO ESCAPE THOSE VILLAINS.
LET'S HAVE A LOOK AT THAT PACKET, JIM.
YES, SIR.

TRELAWNEY UNWRAPPED THE OILSKIN. INSIDE WAS A SHIP'S RECORD BOOK AND A LARGE, MYSTERIOUS CHART.
GRACIOUS! A TREASURE MAP! THIS IS WHAT THE PIRATES WERE AFTER!

THE SQUIRE FELL SILENT, TAPPING HIS DESK AND THINKING.
HMM. I WONDER....
BEFORE HE DIED, BONES SAID HE HAD A TREASURE WORTH MILLIONS. WHAT SHOULD WE DO, SIR?

DO? SIMPLE, MY BOY! I'LL FIND US A SHIP AND WE'LL GO AFTER THE TREASURE OURSELVES!

THE SQUIRE WAS A MAN OF ACTION. WE RETURNED TO THE INN WITH THE BRISTOL SHERIFF TO GUARD US. THEN, A WEEK LATER, THE SQUIRE SENT FOR ME.
THERE SHE IS, JIM. THE GOOD SHIP HISPANIOLA! THE CREW'S BEEN HIRED. YOU'RE COMING AS SHIP'S BOY--AND WE SAIL ON THE MORNING TIDE!
HISPANIOLA

SURE ENOUGH, EARLY THE NEXT MORNING WE WEIGHED ANCHOR AND HEADED FOR TREASURE ISLAND!
SET THE JIB! HARD A-LEE!

LATER, I MET MY SAILING COMPANIONS. CAPTAIN SMOLLETT WAS IN CHARGE OF NAVIGATION.

WELCOME ABOARD!
THANK YOU, SIR.

THE SHIP'S DOCTOR WAS OUR OLD FRIEND, DR. LIVESEY.

--AND THIS, JIM, IS OUR COOK, LONG JOHN SILVER. HE HELPED ME PICK THE CREW.

A SAILOR WITH A MISSING LEG! COULD THIS BE THE VERY ONE BILLY BONES WAS SO AFRAID OF?
HAPPY TO MEET YOU, MATE!
PIECES OF EIGHT!

EXCEPT FOR THE SQUIRE'S PEOPLE, THE CREW WAS A ROUGH, SURLY-LOOKING BUNCH. I WAS PARTICULARLY AFRAID OF ISRAEL HAND, WITH HIS SKULL TATTOO AND SCARRED FACE. I WAS AFRAID TO TURN MY BACK ON THEM.

CAPTAIN SMOLLETT FELT THE SAME WAY. SEVERAL DAYS LATER, AFTER WE WERE FAR OUT TO SEA...
I DON'T TRUST THE CREW, DOCTOR. THEY'RE A PACK OF VILLAINS FOR SURE!
HMM. LET'S KEEP OUR GUNS AND POWDER LOCKED UP.

BEFORE LONG, THE CAPTAIN'S FEARS WERE BORNE OUT. THIS IS HOW IT HAPPENED--

DOCTOR LIVESEY PLACED A BARREL OF APPLES ON THE MAIN DECK.
HELP YOURSELVES, MEN! APPLES WILL KEEP US FROM GETTING SCURVY.

ONE NIGHT, I COULDN'T SLEEP, SO I SLIPPED QUIETLY OUT OF MY BERTH.
I'M HUNGRY FOR AN APPLE!

BY NOW, THE APPLE BARREL WAS ALMOST EMPTY. AS I LEANED WAY OVER TO GET ONE, THE SHIP GAVE A LURCH.
OOPS!

SPRAWLED IN THE BOTTOM OF THE BARREL, I MUST HAVE DOZED OFF. SUDDENLY I HEARD VOICES.
PSST--SILVER! THE MEN ARE GETTING IMPATIENT.

WE'RE READY TO TAKE OVER THE SHIP AND THROW THE SQUIRE AND HIS PALS OVERBOARD!
NOT YET, YOU FOOL.
AWRK
!!

WHY NOT? WE OUTNUMBER THEM EASILY.
WE NEED SMOLLETT TO SAIL THE SHIP AND GET US TO TREASURE ISLAND! THEN WE'LL CRUSH THEM.
LEAVE IT TO ME!
PIECES OF EIGHT!

THEY FINALLY WENT BELOW. I CLIMBED FROM THE BARREL, MY KNEES SHAKING!
THEY'RE PLANNING MURDER! I MUST WARN THE SQUIRE!

BEFORE DAWN THE NEXT MORNING, I MET WITH THE CAPTAIN, THE SQUIRE, AND DR. LIVESEY. I TOLD THEM THE TERRIBLE NEWS.
MUTINEERS! AND LONG JOHN SILVER'S IN CHARGE! I SUSPECTED IT ALL ALONG!
BAM!

IT'S MY FAULT, GENTLEMEN! I TRUSTED LONG JOHN SILVER! HE SWEET-TALKED ME INTO HIRING THOSE MEN!
WELL, WE STILL HAVE THE GUNS AND POWDER LOCKED UP!
NOW WE NEED A CLEVER PLAN...

FOR SEVERAL DAYS, WE DISCUSSED A PLAN OF ACTION. THEN SUDDENLY--
LAND HO!

EVERYONE RACED ON DECK, JABBERING WITH EXCITEMENT!
LAND, MATES! LOOKS MIGHTY GOOD!
IT'S TREASURE ISLAND, JIM! I RECOGNIZE SPYGLASS HILL FROM THE MAP!

BEFORE THE CREW COULD LAY A HAND ON US, CAPTAIN SMOLLETT PUT OUR PLAN INTO ACTION.

SILVER, YOU AND THE MEN DID A FINE JOB WORKING THE SHIP. NOW YOU CAN GO ASHORE FOR THE DAY, AND TAKE SOME RUM.
ER--FINE, SIR! AYE, AYE!
PIECES OF EIGHT! PIECES OF EIGHT!

ALL OF SILVER'S MEN CHOSE TO GO ASHORE, EAGER TO EXPLORE THE ISLAND.
PULL, MY LADS! WE'LL CELEBRATE!
HISPANIOLA

WHILE THEY WERE ASHORE GUZZLING DOWN THEIR RUM, WE RAN TO THE ONE REMAINING BOAT AND LOADED IT WITH OUR WEAPONS AND SUPPLIES.
QUICKLY, QUICKLY!
EASY WITH THOSE MUSKETS, TOM!

HIDDEN FROM THEIR VIEW, WE HEADED FOR SHORE. BUT TWO OF THE PIRATES HAD BEEN SNORING BELOW DECKS.
THEY'RE ESCAPING WITH THE MAP!
LOAD THE BIG GUN!

SUDDENLY A CANNONBALL WHISTLED PAST OUR EARS!
THEY'RE FIRING THE SHIP'S GUN!
PULL HARD FOR SHORE!
BOOM!
SPLASH!

WE STRAINED WITH ALL OUR MIGHT AND REACHED LAND JUST BEFORE ANOTHER SHOT SMASHED OUR BOAT TO SMITHEREENS!
ACCORDING TO THIS MAP, THERE'S AN OLD STOCKADE BEYOND THAT HILL!
HURRY, LADS! THOSE CANNON SHOTS WILL PUT SILVER'S GANG ON OUR TRAIL!
BOOM!

THE PIRATES WHO BURIED THE TREASURE HAD BUILT A STURDY STOCKADE. IT WAS A BIT RUN DOWN, BUT STILL STANDING. WITH THE THREE CREWMEN WHO STAYED LOYAL TO CAPTAIN SMOLLETT, WE WERE SEVEN AGAINST FIFTEEN.
WE'RE OUTNUMBERED! BUT WE'VE GOT PLENTY OF FOOD AND FRESH WATER.
WITH A BIT OF LUCK, I THINK WE CAN DEFEND THIS PLACE!

WHILE THE OTHERS SETTLED IN, THEY SENT ME OUT FOR FIREWOOD.

SOON, IN THE DIMNESS, I SPIED A STRANGE, RAGGED FIGURE DARTING BETWEEN THE TREES!
WHAT IN THE WORLD!?

WAS HE A PIRATE? WAS HE A SPY FOR LONG JOHN SILVER? WITHOUT THINKING, I RAN AFTER HIM!
STOP!
GASP

UGH!
OOF!
THUD

WHY, YOU WEREN'T ON OUR SHIP! W-WHO ARE YOU, ANYWAY?
BEN GUNN'S THE NAME, LAD. POOR BEN GUNN! I HAVEN'T SPOKEN TO ANOTHER HUMAN FOR NIGH ON THREE YEARS!

HALTINGLY, BEN GUNN TOLD ME HIS STORY....
I WAS WITH CAP'N FLINT WHEN HE FIRST BURIED THE TREASURE HERE. FLINT WAS A CRUEL BRUTE. HE DIDN'T LIKE ME. SO WHEN THEY SAILED, HE LEFT ME BEHIND.

I TOOK THE POOR FELLOW TO THE STOCKADE, WHERE HE REPEATED HIS STORY.
I'M A CHANGED MAN, SQUIRE. LET ME JOIN YOU! I'LL FIGHT THOSE VILLAINS GLADLY.
HMM--WE CAN USE ANOTHER HAND. I'LL GIVE YOU A CHANCE.

SUDDENLY, THERE WAS A CRACK FROM A MUSKET! THE BULLET JUST MISSED SQUIRE TRELAWNEY!
THOSE RATS MUST HAVE SMUGGLED GUNS ABOARD!

QUICKLY, WE SPRANG TO DEFEND THE STOCKADE!
TAKE THE EAST WINDOW, JIM! LOOK SHARP!
AYE, AYE, SIR!

URGED ON BY THE WICKED LONG JOHN SILVER, THE BUCCANEERS BEGAN THEIR VICIOUS ATTACK!
FINISH THEM OFF, LADS! THEN THE TREASURE WILL BE OURS! ALL OURS!
CRACK!
PIECES OF EIGHT! PIECES OF EIGHT!

My knees were shaking, and my mouth was dry, but I tried to do my part bravely like the others....

CRACK!

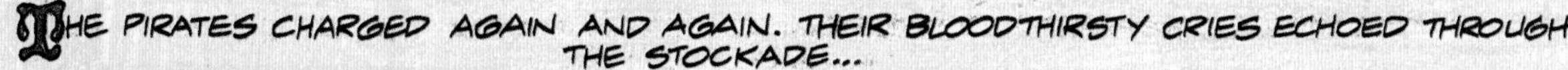
The pirates charged again and again. Their bloodthirsty cries echoed through the stockade...

WHACK!

...But our party fought with courage, beating them off time after time!
BAM!
CRACK!

FINALLY THEY WITHDREW, DRAGGING THEIR WOUNDED, AND WE COULD REST.
TOM REDRUTH'S DEAD, SQUIRE. AND THE CAPTAIN'S BEEN WOUNDED.
TERRIBLE, TERRIBLE! BUT THEY LOST AT LEAST FOUR.
WELL, WE'RE STILL OUTNUMBERED-- AND THEY'LL BE BACK SOON.

WE FOUGHT OFF WAVE AFTER WAVE OF THEIR ATTACKS FOR SEVERAL DAYS. THEN, ONE MORNING, I HAD A WILD, HAREBRAINED SCHEME.
THE SHIP! IT'S OUR ONLY HOPE!

BEN GUNN'S LITTLE HOMEMADE BOAT WAS MOORED NEARBY. I SNEAKED FROM THE FORT AND HOPPED ABOARD.
I'LL CUT THE HISPANIOLA'S ANCHOR. THE TIDE WILL CARRY IT TO OUR SIDE OF THE ISLAND, AND WE CAN USE THE DECK GUN!

HARDLY DARING TO BREATHE, I CLIMBED ABOARD AND WENT TO WORK ON THE ANCHOR CABLE.

THEN...
STOP YOU LITTLE RAT!
ISRAEL HAND!

THE BUCCANEER HAD BEEN ASLEEP BELOWDECKS!
GET AWAY FROM THAT ANCHOR ROPE!

THE HUGE BRUTE RUSHED AT ME WITH HIS DEADLY CUTLASS! TERRIFIED, I LEAPED FOR THE RIGGING!

UP I SCRAMBLED, WITH THE PIRATE CLOSE BEHIND ME!
COME NO CLOSER!
YOU DOG!

HE HURLED HIS CUTLASS AT ME, AND IT NICKED MY SHOULDER! AT THE SAME MOMENT, BOTH MY PISTOLS FIRED...
BAM! BAM!

...AND HAND'S LIFELESS BODY DROPPED INTO THE SEA!

SHAKING IN EVERY LIMB, I CLIMBED DOWN TO THE DECK TO RELOAD MY PISTOLS.

BUT BEFORE I COULD...
WELL, WELL! LOOK, MATES. WE HAVE A VISITOR.
LONG JOHN SILVER!
PIECES OF EIGHT!

JEERING, THEY GRABBED MY PISTOLS AND TIED MY TREMBLING ARMS.

THEN THEY DRAGGED ME TO THE STOCKADE AND, UNDER A FLAG OF TRUCE, BARGAINED WITH MY FRIENDS.
IT'S AN EVEN TRADE. YOU HAND OVER THE MAP, AND WE'LL HAND OVER JIM. OTHERWISE HE WALKS THE PLANK!
YOU GIVE US NO CHOICE, YOU VILLAIN! HERE'S THE MAP. NOW SET JIM FREE.

OF COURSE WE'LL SET THE BOY FREE--AFTER WE GET OUR GOLD!
HAW, HAW, HAW!

PULLING ME ALONG, THE PIRATES RACED TOWARD THE TREASURE SHOWN ON THE MAP.
IT'S JUST BEYOND THESE TREES, LADS!
I C-CAN'T BELIEVE THE OTHERS WOULD ABANDON ME LIKE THIS! I'VE BEEN BETRAYED!

SUDDENLY THEY STOPPED AND GAPED IN ASTONISHMENT.
IT'S GONE! THE GOLD IS G-GONE!
SOMEBODY BEAT US TO IT!

FURIOUS, THE MEN TURNED ON THEIR LEADER!
NOW, LADS, S-STAY CALM!
KILL HIM! KILL THE BOY, TOO!
IT'S ALL YOUR FAULT, SILVER, FOR GETTING US INTO THIS MESS!

THEY RUSHED TOWARD US, MURDER IN THEIR EYES. THEN A SHOT RANG OUT.
CRACK!

STAND WHERE YOU ARE! DROP YOUR CUTLASSES! ONE FALSE MOVE, AND WE FIRE!

SQUIRE, I THOUGHT YOU'D DESERTED ME!
OF COURSE NOT, LAD! WE'VE BEEN CLOSE BEHIND YOU. BEN GUNN DUG UP THE TREASURE LONG AGO.
AND NOW I'M GOING TO SHARE IT WITH ALL OF YOU.

WELL, THERE ISN'T MUCH MORE TO TELL. WE LEFT THE MUTINEERS BEHIND WITH PLENTY OF FOOD AND SUPPLIES. BUT WE TOOK LONG JOHN SILVER WITH US TO STAND TRIAL.

WITH THE TREASURE SAFELY ON BOARD, THE HISPANIOLA MADE A SMOOTH TRIP HOME. BUT BEFORE WE COULD BRING HIM TO JUSTICE, SILVER--THE SLY VILLAIN--JUMPED SHIP AND ESCAPED!
GOOD RIDDANCE, IF YOU ASK ME!

NOW I'M BACK AT THE ADMIRAL BENBOW WITH MOTHER. WE'RE RICH AND CONTENTED. BUT, TO THIS DAY, IN MY WORST DREAMS I CAN STILL HEAR THE SURF BOOMING ON THE COAST OF THAT ACCURSED ISLAND, AND THE SHARP VOICE OF A PARROT RINGING IN MY EARS...
PIECES OF EIGHT! PIECES OF EIGHT!
THE END

ROBERT LOUIS STEVENSON

ROBERT LOUIS STEVENSON, A SCOTTISH AUTHOR AND POET, IS KNOWN FOR HIS EXCITING WORKS OF ADVENTURE. STEVENSON WAS BORN ROBERT LEWIS BALFOUR STEVENSON ON NOVEMBER 13, 1850, IN EDINBURGH, SCOTLAND. STEVENSON WAS SICK WITH TUBERCULOSIS, A LUNG DISEASE, WHEN HE WAS YOUNG, AND HE SPENT MUCH TIME IN BED, WRITING STORIES AND READING. IN 1867, HE WENT TO COLLEGE TO STUDY ENGINEERING, BUT HE HAD TO LEAVE BECAUSE OF HIS POOR HEALTH. HE THEN BEGAN STUDYING LAW. AT THIS TIME, HOWEVER, HE WAS ALSO PUBLISHING SHORT STORIES, ESSAYS, AND ARTICLES ON TRAVEL, BASED ON TRIPS TO EUROPE. AFTER FINISHING HIS LAW STUDIES, HE CONTINUED TRAVELING AND WRITING. HE MARRIED FANNY VANDEGRIFFT OSBOURNE IN 1880, AND THE COUPLE MOVED BACK TO SCOTLAND. HE BEGAN PUBLISHING CHAPTERS OF **TREASURE ISLAND** IN A MAGAZINE IN 1880 AND FINALLY PUBLISHED THE CHAPTERS AS A COMPLETE NOVEL IN 1883. MANY PEOPLE LOVED THIS ADVENTURE TALE. HE SOON FOLLOWED THIS WORK WITH OTHERS, INCLUDING **THE STRANGE CASE OF DR. JEKYLL AND MR. HYDE** (1886) AND **KIDNAPPED** (1886). IN 1890, HE LEFT SCOTLAND FOR THE WARMER WEATHER OF THE SOUTH PACIFIC ISLANDS, IN HOPES THAT THE BETTER WEATHER WOULD HELP IMPROVE HIS HEALTH. STEVENSON LIVED FOUR MORE YEARS BEFORE HE DIED IN 1894, IN HIS HOME IN VAILIMA, SAMOA.